SOCIAL WORK DURING WAR

HUMANITARIAN RESPONSE IN CONFLICT AND WAR SITUATIONS

ASIM KHAN

Dedicated to the memory of my late father

Sh. Khan Kaleem Zahidi

The book is dedicated to my father Sh. Khan Kaleem Zahidi who always motivated me to study more and get more education. He may or may not have solutions to all my life issues, but he made sure hear them out and have a discussion around it.

Though without him, my life has taken its course, but his words of encouragement remain with me. He was a strongly built man with lots of courage and sharp memory. Many a times I was amazed with the fact that he could recall events that happened years ago, and he was also good with remembering names.

With his strong wrist and forearms, he could have carried anything, he rather chose to pick the responsibility of his family. He was a dedicated family man, who totally devoted his life to fulfil the needs of his family to the best he could. He was a dear child to his mother, and I would always admire him for the way he loved and respected his mother.

No matter how much I regret the dreadful day of his sad demise, but as a human being, one must make peace with the fact that one fine day, we all will leave this world for another journey, and may be start from the beginning somewhere else, who knows. I sincerely wish and request everyone reading this book to remember him in their prayers.

Dedicated to the memory of my late grandmother

Smt. Zahida Khanam

It would be hard for me to take this forward without remembering my late grandmother Zahida Khanam. I would like to thank her for encouraging me to chance my endeavours and for all her guidance since my childhood. This book is also dedicated to her along with my father because she made me believe that one should always be in a quest to get educated and learn more. She herself was well educated and used teach in a government school, she had high regards for achieving and spreading knowledge. For me, she always has been synonymous to courage and strength. She would always be in our prayers.

Contents

Foreword

The book offer a poignant and insightful exploration of the critical role of social work during times of war and conflict. As the world grapples with ongoing conflicts and humanitarian crises, the demand for compassionate and skilled social workers has never been greater. This book sheds light on the challenges, ethical dilemmas, and triumphs of social workers who dedicate their lives to alleviating suffering and promoting human dignity in the midst of war.

The chapters within delve into a range of topics, from the psychological impact of war on individuals and communities to the practical challenges of delivering social services in conflict zones. The author draw on their own experience and the latest research to provide a comprehensive overview of the field.

As you read through these pages, you will gain a deeper understanding of the complex and often heartbreaking realities faced by social workers in war zones. You will also be inspired by their unwavering commitment to helping others, even in the most difficult of circumstances.

I encourage you to share this book with others, to raise awareness of the crucial role of social work in times of war, and to inspire future generations of compassionate professionals to make a difference.

Let us hope that the lessons learned from the past can inform the future and help to create a more peaceful and just world.

Acknowledgements

I would like to thank my family and friends for their patience, understanding, and encouragement throughout this process. Their love and support have been invaluable.

Finally, I would like to dedicate this book to the countless social workers who have dedicated their lives to helping others, especially those affected by war and conflict. Their courage, compassion, and resilience inspire us all.

Prologue

War, a scourge on humanity, leaves an indelible mark on individuals and societies. It erodes the fabric of communities, uproots lives, and sows seeds of trauma. In the midst of chaos and destruction, social workers emerge as beacons of hope, offering a lifeline to those in need.

This book delves into the critical role of social work in times of war and conflict. It explores the challenges, triumphs, and ethical dilemmas faced by social workers as they navigate the complexities of humanitarian crises. From providing immediate relief to facilitating long-term recovery, social workers are at the forefront of responding to the human cost of war.

Through the lens of theory and practice, this book examines the multifaceted nature of social work during war. It explores the psychological impact of trauma, the importance of cultural competence, and the ethical considerations involved in working with vulnerable populations.

As you embark on this journey, you will encounter stories of resilience, compassion, and the enduring human spirit. These narratives highlight the transformative power of social work and its potential to heal and rebuild shattered lives.

Preface

Amidst war and conflict, humanity is often pushed to the brink. The devastating impact of war on individuals, communities, and societies cannot be overstated. However, even in the darkest of times, there are beacons of hope. International and local NGOs have been at the forefront of humanitarian response in conflict zones, providing critical aid, support, and protection to those affected.

This book aims to shine a light on the remarkable work of these NGOs, highlighting their contributions to the rescue and aid efforts in war-torn areas. From providing mental health support to army personnel to assisting refugees who have been forced to flee their homes, the stories of courage, resilience, and compassion that emerge from these efforts are a testament to the human spirit.

Through this book, I hope to raise awareness about the critical role that NGOs play in responding to humanitarian crises, and to inspire others to join forces in promoting peace, justice, and human dignity. I also hope to provide a platform for the voices and stories of those who have been impacted by war, and to honor the selfless work of the NGOs and individuals who are dedicated to making a difference.

It is my sincere hope that this book will serve as a reminder of the power of humanity and compassion, even in the face of adversity.

Author
Mohammad Asim Khan

CHAPTER I

INTRODUCTION

Relief operations relate to the philanthropic aid or backing given to people in torture by individualities, associations, or governments with the core purpose of precluding and easing mortal suffering.

The principles of philanthropic intervention are equity, impartiality, and independence. Equity means no demarcation on the base of nation, race, religious beliefs, class, gender, or political opinions philanthropic interventions are guided by requirements. Neutrality demands that philanthropic agencies don't take sides in either conflict or ideological contestation. Independence requires that philanthropic agencies retain their autonomy of action. These principles, firstly drawn up for war and consolidated in philanthropic law expressed in the Geneva Convention of 1949, uphold response to conflict- related and natural disasters.

Since the early 1990s, there has been both an increase in the number of disasters and a change in extremities, therefore leading to a substantial increase in relief operations. Natural disasters have grown in number largely due to increased climate variability. Complex extremities (situations of fortified conflict) have increased, particularly since the end of the Cold War, and are now characterized by high situations of mercenary casualties, deliberate destruction of livelihoods and weal systems, collapse of the rule of law, and large figures of displaced people. According to the United Nations High Commission for Deportees (UNHCR), there were 8.4 million deportees and 23.7

million internally displaced persons (IDPs) as of December 2005.

Extremities have changed in nature from generally natural disasters, dominated by flood tide and failure, to complex extremities and technological disasters. The 'War on Terror' following events on 11 September 2001 and the posterior interventions in Afghanistan and Iraq have created new challenges for the perpetration of relief operations.

The adding frequency and changing face of extremities have caused philanthropic expenditures to soar. Total philanthropic backing reached an each- time high in 2005 at around US$ 18 billion – the Asian riffle alone mustered an unknown response. In real terms, philanthropic aid from the Organization for Economics-operation and Development (OECD) Development Assistance Committee (DAC) members rose by 32 in 2005. DAC is a forum of major bilateral benefactors with 23 members, including the Commission of the European Communities and the United States.) These numbers do not regard for charitable donations from individualities or groups, similar as churches, and they do not capture non-Western backing similar as that handed by Islamic realities.

The transnational philanthropic system consists, basically, of four sets of actors patron governments, including the European Commission Humanitarian Office (ECHO), the United Nations (UN), the International Red Cross and Red Crescent Movement, and transnational nongovernmental associations (INGOs). Original NGOs and heirs have little voice in the system.

A broad division of labor exists within the United Nations system. The Office for the Collaboration of Humanitarian Assistance (OCHA) is in charge of the policy and planning frame; World Food Program (WFP) is responsible for exigency food delivery; the United Nations High Commission for Deportees (UNHCR) is in charge of exigency sanctum; United Nations Children Fund (UNICEF) is responsible for nutrition and water and sanitation; and the Food and Agricultural Organization (FAO) is responsible for exigency husbandry, which if successful should mark the end of the exigency and the depression of the part of the WFP.

Ironically, the health sector is the only sector not delivered directly by the UN. That rests largely with the International Committee of the Red Cross (ICRC) and Médecins Sans Frontiers (MSF), who arguably are the only two absolute philanthropic associations. The World Health Organization (WHO) is generally involved with programming and policy, lower involved with the operation of medical delivery, and not at all involved in medical delivery. Despite this there are three distinct areas in which the UN delivers what can astronomically be described as medical interventions. These are food security (including nutrition), sanctum, and water and sanitation.

On-the-ground operation of relief remains a contentious subject and is nearly tied to the issue of collaboration. The United Nations system, through OCHA, is generally responsible for the collaboration of ground- position operation, decreasingly through the 'Cluster Approach' in which agencies are linked to lead collaboration in a specific sector. In places where the United Nations isn't respectable, the ICRC plays the critical collaboration part. Utmost disaster prayers are underfunded so the philanthropic system generally has inadequate coffers to deliver the applicable philanthropic response. As a result, utmost NGOs agree to be coordinated through the UN system.

When disaster prayers are met or exceeded, as in the Asian Riffle, the different United Nations agencies and transnational NGOs tend to work more singly. Coherent and effective on- the- ground operation relies eventually on the honest sharing of information about devisee need and content. FAO has handed a model of good practice for this by chairing information participating through its food security assessment unit (FSAU). In general, still, information sharing for on- the- ground operation, and thus effective collaboration, remains the weakest link in philanthropic delivery.

CHAPTER II

ROLE OF PHILANTHROPY

Since the early 1990s, there has been both an increase in the number of disasters and a change in extremities leading to a substantial increase in philanthropic backing. Extremities have changed in nature from substantially being natural disasters similar as cataracts, dearth's, and famines to complex extremities similar as the 'war on terror'post-11 September 2001, and the interventions in Afghanistan and Iraq have created new challenges for the perpetration of philanthropic backing. Due to climatic changes, natural disasters have grown in number, for illustration, cataracts, hurricanes, typhoons, and famines. Since the end of the Cold War, complex extremities especially violent conflicts have increased, which are characterized by the collapse of the rule of law, destruction of livelihoods, and relegation of people. All these complex extremities are brought into the public limelight by the transnational media, which has led to significant mindfulness among people. The World Disasters Report in 2001 estimated that in the 10 times (1991 – 2000), 2.3 million people lost their lives in conflict situations. The adding frequency and changing face of extremities has caused philanthropic expenditure to rise to an all-time high of US$ 7.8 billion in 2003. This figure does not record the number of charitable donations from individualities or groups or of nonwestern backing of colorful kinds, including those from religious associations.

Philanthropic aid is the backing given to people in torture by individualities, associations, or governments with the core purpose of precluding and easing mortal suffering. Philanthropic interventions are principally guided by requirements, but it follows three main principles of philanthropic law as expressed in the Geneva Convention of 1949 emphasizing equity, impartiality, and independence. Equity means no demarcation on the base of nation, race, religious beliefs, class, gender, or political opinions. Neutrality demands that philanthropic agencies do n't take sides in either conflict or ideological contestation. Independence requires that philanthropic agencies retain their autonomy of action.

The Collaboration of Humanitarian Assistance (OCHA), on behalf of the United Nations, provides leadership and coordinates the prompt and smooth delivery of relief backing. It's supported by the World Food Programme (WFP) responsible for exigency food delivery; the United Nations High Commission for Deportees (UNHCR) responsible for sanctum; the United Nations Children Fund (UNICEF) responsible for nutrition and water and sanitation; and the Food and Agricultural Organization (FAO) responsible for food and exigency husbandry, while the Red Cross and transnational NGOs like Merlin give medical interventions.

Philanthropic aid is substantially a short- term intervention to give relief. The transition from relief to recuperation and development is delicate and the long-term aspects of development need to be assessed with other development agencies from the original phase of furnishing relief. In some countries – Angola, Sierra Leone, Somalia, to name a many – philanthropic aid was handed over a long period, but the system is n't equipped for long-term intervention leading to recuperation and development. Benefactors at times have used philanthropic aid to avoid engagement with undemocratic countries and their approaches were frequently driven by political interest rather than according to the need.

Philanthropic operations are now accompanied by military interventions (peace- keeping operations) especially in the last two decades in the environment of violent conflicts. These have been nominated as complex political extremities (e.g., East Timor, Kosovo, and Burundi). The World Bank has therefore placed considerable emphasis on responding to conflict, particularly where it notes that one- fifth of Africans now live in countries oppressively disintegrated by conflict. These have accompanied proliferation of small arms and landmines and particularly sexual violence and exploitation of women and children leading to high threat of HIV/ AIDS. In 2003, three million people failed of HIV/ AIDS and it's turning into a large- scale disaster. The UNHCR, in 2006, recorded that there were 8.4 million deportees worldwide (31 in Africa and 36 in Asia) and 23.7 million internally displaced persons (IDPs), who were n't only displaced from their home but also their livelihoods.

According to the UNHCR, in 2006, there were also a farther 688000 shelter- campaigners substantially in Europe and North America – who had claimed exile status but whose claims were not yet honored. In Sudan, it's estimated that further than 400 000 people have been killed and 2.5 million have been displaced in the genocide in Darfur. In 2005, world military expenditure totaled to $1118 billion, of which 47 was reckoned for by the US. The response to terrorist attacks in the west, known as the 'war on terror', has also led to increase of expenditure.

All these events pose new challenges to the impartiality of philanthropic action and the aid workers themselves.

The rise of terrorism and the range of counterterrorism enterprise by governments have also generated new protection issues especially in relation to mortal right laws. Can philanthropic backing be independent of foreign aid policy in the contemporary world. numerous questions are raised regarding the responsibility and performance of aid agencies and United Nations OCHA, as the supereminent global philanthropic agencies are heavily blamed for poor performance. On the other hand, if we didn't have an effective coordinating agency like the OCHA, we'd not be suitable to give relief and backing at all. Since 1996, the philanthropic sector has accepted numerous enterprises to ameliorate responsibility and performance similar as the good philanthropic donorship action to ensure that benefactors' responses are indifferent, effective, and harmonious with the philanthropic principles as explained over. The philanthropic agencies have developed the active learning network and the philanthropic responsibility partnership.

CHAPTER III

PROFESSIONAL SOCIAL WORK

What is Professional Social Work?

What is the most appropriate definition of contemporary social work? Competing definitions of social work vie for acceptance. This chapter provides an initial understanding of what social work aspires to be, how the British social work degree is constructed, and why the caring services need professional social work. Social work changes and adapts to new social concerns and organisational structures, so that contemporary social work is characterised by its changing nature, rather than its agreement on a specific definition. Ever since social work began to evolve as a distinct profession, its definition has been debated. There is a basic need for a practical definition to better explain the profession to itself, the public, and policy makers. Emerging from a two-pronged approach-intervention with individuals and at the community level-social work is now a recognized and licensed profession. Ultimately, one could argue, as Richmond (1917) did, that the profession of social work is defined every day in hundreds of thousands of ways by individuals with the title of social worker by who they are and what they do. Central to a definition, as Bartlett (1958) noted, are the core ingredients of values, purpose, sanction, knowledge, and method.

Understanding the conceptual social work

"Social work is the professional activity of helping individuals, groups, or communities enhance or restore their capacity for social functioning and creating social conditions favorable to this goal" (NASW, 1973). This statement provides a concise one –sentence "dictionary definition" of the profession. It draws important boundaries around social work. First, social work is considered as a professional activity. Professional activity requires a particular body of knowledge, values, and skills as well as a discrete purpose that guides one's practice activities. When practice is judged professional, community sanction to perform these tasks is assumed to be present, and the profession, in turn, is expected to be accountable to the public for the quality of services provided. Therefore, the definition implies social work has fulfilled these requirements.

Second, the definition captures the uniqueness of social work. It makes clear that social workers serve a range of client system that include individuals, families, or other household units, groups, organizations, neighborhoods', communities, and even larger unities of society. For social work, identification of one client system is difficult because client or target of practice activity may range from an individual to a state or a nation. The unique activities of social workers are directed towards helping all those systems interact more effectively and require professional education as preparation. Katherine Kendall (1978) argues that the uniqueness of social work as a professional activity rests on its capacity to: Assess the nature of the need and the problem, to estimate the capacity of the person to handle the problem, to foster every inner strength of the person toward the goal of finding his own solution and to utilize all the outer resources of the environment and the community which might be of value in this problem-solving endeavor.

Finally, the last part of the definition concerns social workers dual focus on person and environment. Social workers help people enhance or restore their capacity for social functioning. At the same time, they work to change societal conditions that may help or hinder people from improving their social functioning. Here lies another uniqueness of social work. Its concern with the fit between individuals and their social circumstances is a distinctive characteristic of social work and provides its foundation as a discipline. When working with clients, social workers must take into consideration both the characteristics of the person and the impinging forces from the environment.

Social workers operate at the boundary between people and their environment. Whereas some professions focus on changing the person and others on changing the environment, social works attention is directed to the connection between person and environment. In contrast, the physician is primarily prepared to treat physical aspects of the individual, and the attorney is largely concerned with the operation of the legal system in the larger environment (although both the physician and attorney should give secondary attention to other, related systems). Social work recognizes that each person brings to the helping situation a set of behaviors, needs, and beliefs that are the result of his or her unique experiences from birth. Yet it also recognizes that whatever is brought to the situation must be related to the world as that person confronts it. By focusing on transactions between the person and his or her environment, social interaction can be improved. In sum, social workers temporarily enter the lives of their clients to help them improve their transactions with important elements of their environment.

Social work is a professional and academic discipline committed to the pursuit of social welfare and social change. It is a field of study that has uniquely blended perspectives from other disciplines, particularly the biological and social sciences, with its own values, knowledge, and skills. Education for the profession requires foundational understanding of human needs, social problems, social welfare responses, consumers of social services and professional interventions as well as developing skills to facilitate change and assimilating a social work value orientation. In short, students, early in their educational experience, want to know who, what and the why of social work.

Social work is a profession charged with fulfilling the social welfare mandate of promoting wellbeing and quality of life. Thus, social work encompasses activities directed at improving human and social conditions and alleviating human distress and social problems. Social workers, as caring professionals, work with people to enhance their competence and functioning, to access social supports and resources, to create humane and responsive social services and to expand the structures of society that provide opportunities for all citizens. Social work profession exists to provide humane and effective social service to individuals, families, groups, communities, and society so that social functioning may be enhanced and the qualities of life improved. It is an activity that seeks to help individuals, families, groups, organisations and communities engage resources that will alleviate human problems.

In essence, social work activities empower client systems to enhance their competence and enable social structures to relieve human suffering and remedy social problems. Social work is concerned, too, with enabling clients to develop capacities and strengths that will improve their social functioning. Social work in its various forms addresses the multiple, complex transactions between people and their environments. Its mission is to enable all people to develop their full potential, enrich their lives, and prevent dysfunction. Professional social work is focused on problem solving and change. Social work is an active, "doing" profession that brings about positive change in problem situations through problem solving or prevention. As such, social workers are change agents in society and in the lives of the individuals, families, and communities they serve.

A helping profession: Social work is a profession focused on enhancing human well-being and addressing the complex needs of individuals, families, and communities. Social work is aptly called a "helping profession" in India due to its fundamental nature and the significant impact it has on individuals, families, and communities. Here's why:

Direct assistance and support:

- **Individual Counselling:** Social workers provide one-on-one counselling and therapy to help individuals cope with personal challenges, mental health issues, and life transitions.
- **Family Counselling:** They work with families to address relationship problems, conflicts, and crises, promoting healthier family dynamics.
- **Group Therapy:** Social workers facilitate group therapy sessions where individuals can share experiences, learn from others, and develop coping strategies.

Empowerment and Advocacy:

- **Community Organizing:** Social workers mobilize communities to address social issues, advocate for their rights, and create positive change.
- **Policy Advocacy:** They work to influence social policies and legislation to improve the lives of vulnerable populations.
- **Empowerment:** Social workers empower individuals and communities to take control of their lives, make informed decisions, and achieve their goals.

Resource coordination and case management:

- **Connecting to Services:** Social workers help individuals and families access essential services like healthcare, housing, education, and legal aid.
- **Case Management:** They coordinate and monitor the delivery of services to ensure that clients receive the support they need.

Social justice and change:

- **Addressing Inequality:** Social workers work to address systemic issues like poverty, discrimination, and social injustice.
- **Promoting Human Rights:** They advocate for the rights of marginalized and oppressed groups.

Where do professional social workers work?
Social workers can be found in a wide range of settings, including:

- **Healthcare:** Hospitals, clinics, mental health facilities
- **Social Services:** Child welfare agencies, family service agencies, senior centers
- **Education:** Schools, colleges, universities
- **Government:** State and federal agencies, non-profit organizations
- **Criminal Justice:** Prisons, juvenile detention centers, probation offices
- **Military:** Supporting military personnel and their families

Social work's search for a definition was prompted by its quest to attain professional status.

Leading figures in the development of social work after the Second World War asked:

Ques 1. What is social work?

Ques 2. Is social work a profession?

The answer to the second question is now more evidently 'yes', but the search for professional status is not yet concluded. Higher expectations of social work pose a challenge for social workers. Social work practitioners themselves will validate social work's claim to be a profession as they develop their professional practice to the high standards required by the social work degree and by their post qualification studies. Whether you, the reader, are a social work student on a degree programme or an experienced practitioner, you will be (or will become) familiar with the climate of change that challenges social work's ability to respond. Social workers have to grapple with new social issues and dilemmas that affect the lives of people seeking help. To function at that level of practice, they have to be well informed and confident in their professional ability to exercise appropriate judgments.

Social Work, Helping Professions, Caring Services and the Welfare State Social work is located within a network of caring services or personal social services staffed by members of the helping professions. The term helping profession is self-explanatory. Social work is not the only helping profession (Heraud, 1970). Other helping professions include the well accepted roles of nursing, teaching, and medicine. Social workers practise alongside other professional and vocational workers in a range of service provision designated as the caring services. The term 'caring services' is an imperfect description of the service provision delivered by different organisational structures (Tossell and Webb, 1994). Not all of these organisations are overtly 'caring'. History determines their inclusion on the list. Beveridge identified five giants (want, ignorance, idleness, disease, and squalor) that had to be overcome through establishment of the range of comprehensive services that are known as the welfare state.

Social Work has a recognised practice expertise since 1991, well-established post-qualification programmes, including the Practice Teaching Award, the Post Qualifying Award in Child Care, and the Mental Health Social Worker Award (General Social Care Council [GSCC], 2001), demonstrate achievement of recognised practice expertise. Post-qualification study following the degree in social work will enhance social workers' skills and specialist expertise. Social Work Has Restricted Entry through Qualifications Universities and colleges offering social work education have a tradition of requiring qualifications for entry, including non-standard qualifications of previous life experience, experience in social care, and access to higher education courses as well as conventional academic qualifications. Social work education traditionally has interviewed applicants to ensure a sound selection for the profession.

Why Choose Social Work?

Social work offers the opportunity to make a real difference in people's lives and contribute to positive social change. Social workers have the opportunity to directly impact people's lives by providing support, guidance, and resources to those in need. This can lead to significant positive changes in individuals, families, and communities. The field of social work offers a wide range of career options, allowing you to find a path that aligns with your interests and skills. You can work in various settings such as hospitals, schools, non-profit organizations, government agencies, and more. Social work challenges you to develop strong interpersonal skills, critical thinking, problem-solving abilities, and empathy. You'll learn to understand complex social issues and work effectively with diverse populations. This personal growth can be incredibly rewarding. Social workers are often at the forefront of social justice movements, advocating for policies that improve the lives of marginalized groups. You can contribute to positive change in society and make a lasting impact. Witnessing the positive impact of your work on individuals and communities can be deeply fulfilling. Seeing people overcome challenges, achieve their goals, and live healthier, happier lives is a powerful motivator.The field of social work offers a wide range of career paths and settings to explore. With increasing social needs, there is a growing demand for skilled social workers

In essence, social work in India is a helping profession because it:

- **Prioritizes human well-being:** Social workers are committed to improving the quality of life for individuals and communities.
- **Addresses diverse needs:** They work with people from all walks of life, addressing a wide range of social issues.
- **Fosters resilience and empowerment:** Social workers equip individuals and communities with the tools they need to overcome challenges and build a better future.

The dedication of social workers to helping others and making a positive impact on society is what truly defines the profession as a helping one.

- **Focus on Vulnerable Populations:** Social workers often work with people who are facing challenges due to poverty, discrimination, mental health issues, substance abuse, or other social injustices.
- **Multi-faceted Approach:** Social workers use a variety of methods to help people, including:

  - **Counselling & Therapy:** Providing individual, family, or group therapy to address emotional and mental health needs.
  - **Case Management:** Coordinating services and resources for clients to ensure they receive the support they need.
  - **Advocacy:** Fighting for social justice and advocating for policies that improve the lives of vulnerable populations.
  - **Community Organizing:** Building and empowering communities to address social issues and create positive change.

- **Policy Analysis:** Researching and analyzing social policies to identify areas for improvement and advocate for change.

CHAPTER IV

HELPFUL MAPPING

Helpful mapping is a social work tool used to identify and visualize the supportive networks and resources available to individuals, families, or communities. It's a collaborative and strengths-based approach that helps social workers:

- **Identify supportive relationships**: Map the people, organizations, and community resources that provide emotional, practical, or financial support.
- **Recognize strengths and resilience**: Highlight the client's coping mechanisms, skills, and abilities that have helped them navigate challenging situations.
- **Develop a support network**: Create a visual representation of the supportive relationships and resources, making it easier to access and utilize them.
- **Foster empowerment and self-advocacy**: Encourage clients to take an active role in identifying and mobilizing their support networks.

Overall, helpful mapping is a valuable tool for social workers to promote well-being, resilience, and empowerment.

The Scope of Helpful Mapping

Although a broader concept based on a standardizing want to make strides human welfare and thriving, compassion, in hone, is to a great extent characterized by a more centered set of exercises, which point to give the necessities of life for bunches in quick require. Compassion is practiced around the world, attempted by nearby, national, and worldwide organizations to address a wide extend of human needs. High-profile issues to which helpful help is coordinated incorporate open wellbeing crises, political emergencies, war, "natural" catastrophes, and constrained relocation. For occurrence, later Ebola infection episodes, the continuous Israel/Palestine strife, the respectful war in Syria, Storm Katrina, and the worldwide displaced person emergency are all cases of large-scale occasions that have required critical compassionate mediation. Reaction to more localized human needs in the setting of occasions such as flooding and rapidly spreading fire alleviation moreover successfully drop beneath the domain of compassion; in any case, the term is generally saved for activities to combat issues of national or worldwide significance.

Mapping and Compassionate Data Management

While much of the consideration is centered on the quick, short-term necessities of a crisis or emergency occasion, there is a much longer transience to compassion activity, and mapping and data administration for the most part are exceedingly imperative all through. The UN's Inter-Agency Compassionate Program Cycle (HPC) freely takes after the four stages of the calamity administration cycle: anticipation, readiness, reaction, and recuperation. The HPC has five stages: (1) needs evaluation and investigation, (2) key reaction arranging, (3) asset mobilization, (4) execution and checking, and (5) operational survey and assessment. This multiphase conceptualization strengthens the require thinking of compassionate mediations past quick needs amid an crisis or emergency occasion. These five stages are supported by two persistent needs, coordination, and data administration; they are central to successful decision-making all through a prepare of planning for, overseeing, and conveying helpful reaction. Maps play a particularly imperative part in compassionate data administration not as it were since of the profoundly geographic nature of helpful issues such as catastrophes or movement but too due to their capacity to quicken evidence-based decision-making through data decrease and rearrangements, a highlight characteristic to all visual shapes of representation (e.g., pictures, charts, and info graphics).

Many set up compassionate organizations such as the Universal League of Ruddy Cross and Ruddy Bow Social orders, The UN Displaced person Organization, and the Joined together Countries Office for the Coordination of Helpful Issues have well-developed mapping and spatial information operations as portion of their data administration commands. Furthermore, little dexterous organizations are able to give custom, profoundly responsive mapping and data administration administrations to make strides situational mindfulness for these bigger organizations. For occurrence, Map Action is a charitable organization that quickly sends prepared GIS specialists to influenced zones in the repercussions of helpful crises, to give spatial information administration administrations and make maps of the spatial setting, nearby administrations and foundation, coordination's, populace defenselessness, dangers, and risks. The GIS Corps, organized by the Urban and Territorial Data Frameworks Affiliation, is a program that conveys GIS and mapping volunteers to underserved places around the world, supporting helpful alleviation as well as broader human rights, financial advancement, environment, and instruction mandates.

Mapping and Computerized Humanitarianism

Mapping has gotten to be indeed more vital inside compassionate data administration in later a long time, as one of the essential devices of the field of "digital humanitarianism," an exertion to lock in the open in helpful arranging and reaction through computerized advances. Computerized compassion rose to noticeable quality in the wake of the annihilating seismic tremor in Haiti in 2010, when several computerized mapping ventures illustrated the conceivable outcomes of broadly conveyed, mass cooperation in spatial information and outline generation to empower fast evidence-based decision-making, particularly for the reaction and recuperation stages. These exercises were made conceivable by modern progressions in advanced mapping, versatile advances, and Web communications, as well as the modern shapes of social hone they enabled.

The development of Web 2.0 in the early to mid-2000s was an imperative minute in the advancement of compassionate mapping. This moment wave of the Web has been portrayed as the point in which the Web got to be a stage for open support, sharing, and substance creation or maybe than fair data recovery, a move that was made conceivable through the development of social media stages, web journal destinations, and video transfer stages. The prospect of user-generated substance delivered on Web clients proclaimed an unused opportunity for helpful mapping, particularly as its spatial appearance, the geospatial Web (Geo Web) started to rise. The appearance of the Geo Web was a turning point in the broader field of GIS and advanced mapping, with companies such as Google entering the geospatial advertise with simple to utilize, frequently free, mapping, and geo visualization stages (e.g., Maps, Soil, and Road See) that were rapidly taken up by individuals of the open and organizations to deliver spatial information and maps for compassionate purposes. The Geo Web, be that as it may, can be more totally caught on as a sociotechnical array, a collection of advances and social hones cohered by the more extensive accessibility of advanced mapping and spatial examination stages online, the improvement of these stages in Web innovation communities or maybe than the customary GIS division, and unused hones rising due to their utilize by normal Web clients in a Web 2.0 sharing setting. The term utilized at the time, neo geography, alluded to the development in non-specialist utilize of online mapping stages to create spatial information and maps driven to a modern category of Web client. These unused improvements hurried the development of crowdsourcing, which itself was central to the development of compassionate mapping. Crowdsourcing alludes to the hone of outsourcing assignments and exercises to the swarm; the swarm can allude to a gather of known members or without a doubt more extensive obscure publics gathered on the Web. In both cases, members regularly contribute to exercises remotely through Web-based stages and portable advances, although on the ground shapes of crowdsourcing ventures are moreover common. Map-based crowdsourcing activities have been a few of the most fruitful and broadly celebrated illustrations. Here, donors include or expand spatial information on Web mapping interfacing, for case, contributing spatial system information (e.g., streets and focuses of interface) or topical spatial information (e.g., traits or occasions related with a particular put). In both cases, venture goals regularly look for to fill information holes or create more up-to-date datasets and maps than what as of now exists, whether the deliberate is to deliver a base outline of a territorial street organize for crisis readiness purposes or the areas of catastrophe harm to help in crisis response.

Open Street Map (OSM)—the open-source crowd sourced advanced outline project—is closely related with the rise in map-focused computerized compassion. OSM was begun in 2004 by Steve Coast with the point of creating spatial information utilizing a collaborative open-source show. OSM outline information are contributed by clients in neighborhood communities and around the world, through following adj. symbolism and uploading GPS tracks and point area information, utilizing a "wiki" commitment and community altering demonstrate comparative to Wikipedia. Significant donor intrigued in the venture has set OSM as a critical source of spatial information. The projects ceaselessly overhauled and made strides advanced outline of the world, in a few cases, has more precise and total scope than items from national mapping organizations or corporate stages counting Google Maps. The information permitting show, at first, Imaginative Commons, and presently, Open Information Commons, has empowered broad utilize of the information by engineers and third parties counting corporate stages, which has assisted stabilized the OSM extend. For helpful purposes, the OSM stage has been broadly utilized since of its edit ability, maps of any given region can be delivered quickly by any neighborhood or disseminated supporters with get to the Web. For occurrence, appears the OSM interface in alter mode, utilizing the coordinates Potlatch 2 editor to outline the Kya Sands Casual Settlement in Johannesburg, South Africa. Kya Sands is domestic to around 20,000 individuals, although it is exceedingly marginalized, underserviced, and not recorded on maps delivered by the state or corporate mapping stages. Several helpful issues are of concern in the community, counting normal fires that annihilate shack lodging. Mapping Kya Sands and other "unmapped" places can upgrade situational mindfulness amid an emergency occasion and lead to way better arranging and readiness to moderate against the dangers of future occasions.

CHAPTER V

THE HUMAN RIGHTS LENS

Many rules of universal human rights law were outlined to constrain viciousness. Standards relating to helpful intercession, the law of war, and rules administering national crises appear the rationale of the worldwide framework with respect to the legitimate administration of conflict.

A perpetual address is: When is intercession by one state in the domain of another defended in arrange to ensure human rights? Most researchers incline toward multilateral intercession to one-sided mediation since they consider it less helpless to mishandle. Undoubtedly, the wrangle about around whether standard worldwide law licenses helpful intercession has been petulant. The ICJ tended to the authenticity of helpful intercession to secure human rights in its 1986 judgment in the Case Concerning Military and Paramilitary Exercises in and Against Nicaragua. The World Court expressed that the utilize of constrain to ensure human rights, in the setting of that case, seem not be advocated beneath universal law. The whole preface appeared illogical and the assurance of human rights, a entirely compassionate objective, cannot be consistent with the mining of ports, the annihilation of oil establishments, or once more with the preparing, equipping and preparing of the contras. The Court concludes that the contention determined from the conservation of human rights in Nicaragua cannot manage a legitimate legitimization for the conduct of the U.S.

As for treaty-based avocation, the Joined together Countries Constitution stipulates in Article 2(7) that the UN might not mediate in "matters which are basically inside the ward of any state" but makes no say of a comparative forbiddance for part states. Article 2(4) forbids the risk or utilize of constrain against the regional keenness or political freedom of any state. It does not say intercession per se. The UN can intercede if a circumstance postures a "threat to the peace" inside the meaning of Article 39 of the Joined together Countries Constitution. Article 42 indicates what steps the UN Security Board may take, such as exhibits, bar, and other operations by discuss, ocean, or arrive powers, in arrange to reestablish worldwide peace and security. The Security Chamber conjured these powers when it forced financial sanctions against Southern Rhodesia in 1968, and arms ban against South Africa in the early 1970s. In the Inlet War, the Security Board depended on Determination 688 (1991), which made a reference to Chapter VII of the UN Constitution, the Council's commitment to keep up worldwide peace and security.

The choice to utilize constrain against another state can be advocated if it is in self-defense. Although less well set up is whether this right can be worked out some time recently an assault happens. The disputable tenet of expectant defense was conjured, for illustration, in 1982, when Israel assaulted a atomic reactor in Iraq. In 2002 the Joined together States depended on a comparable contention; it attacked Iraq claiming this activity was reasonable on the premise of preemptive constrain on the hypothesis that Saddam Hussein had weapons of mass pulverization. Apparently, the qualification between more seasoned convention of expectant self-defense and the more current approach, preemptive constrain, is that the previous included an inescapable danger of up-and-coming harm.

When US strengths did not find any stockpile of weapons in Iraq, the Bush Organization at that point emphasized that Saddam Hussein had committed awful acts counting the utilize of nerve gas against the Kurds, the torment and murdering of Iraqi citizens, and other net infringement of worldwide human rights laws; the plausibility that Iraq was the preparing ground for psychological militants was moreover famous. Whereas there has been considerable documentation of these shocking acts, there was too grave concern around the conduct of US military work force and private temporary workers. The Taguba Report given broad prove of the degree of the mishandle in the Abu Ghraib jail. The infamous photos from the Abu Ghraib jail, uncovering the twisted treatment of those kept interior, stunned the worldwide community. There were moreover archived killings of civilians as in the town of Haditha in Western Iraq in 2005. Media scope of the Haditha killings driven to court Martials beneath the Uniform Code of Military Justice.

In the Iraq war numerous companies provided work force, a few of whom abused universal law. This raised modern questions almost the application of worldwide benchmarks to private military temporary workers. In the Joined together States there was a call for examination into the part of companies such as Blackwater, one which was charged of duty for the passing of civilians. Although Congress had sanctioned laws to clarify the truth that the temporary workers were subject to the Uniform Code of Military Equity (the Military Extraterritorial Jusiction Act), the US government was moderate to implement the pertinent laws.

The Law of War

There are a few degrees of cover between helpful universal law and universal human rights law. The fundamental contrast between the two is that though compassionate law as it were applying amid wartime, worldwide human rights law is continuously in impact. The law of war comprises of standard worldwide law standards dating back centuries. After World War II, states codified the law when they embraced the four Geneva Traditions of 12 Admirable 1949. At first, a few contended that the rules ought to apply to both gracious and worldwide clashes, but in the conclusion, it was chosen that they would not apply to "internal" equipped clashes. A few states were concerned that if the rules connected to inside clashes, this would deliver rebels de facto status as belligerents and conceivably indeed de jure legitimate acknowledgment. Essentially, states did not need to make a instrument that would bestow authenticity on rebels. Since these same states were restricted to giving rebels detainee of war status incompletely since they needed to debilitate disobedience, they induced the discretionary conference to make the rules pertinent as it were to universal outfitted conflicts.

The compromise, which got to be known as the 'Common Article Three' (since it is in all four Geneva Traditions), ensures combatants and civilians amid "non-international conflicts." It sets forward a charge of rights for non-international equipped clashes, and, at the time of its appropriation, was a noteworthy advancement. Since it is not clear absolutely what constitutes "non-international outfitted conflict" and since states stressed that rebels would pick up universal lawful status as belligerents if

Common Article Three is connected to their inner clashes, the arrangement has not had the down to earth victory desired.

In the late 1970s there was an endeavor to grow Common Article Three through two Extra Conventions (1977). Convention 1 managed with the marvel of anticolonial clashes, so-called wars of national freedom. It was planned to recognize the universal character of wars of national freedom based on the right of self-determination, a right so imperative that it shows up as Article 1 in both the ICCPR and the ICECSR. Western countries went without when the last vote was taken, with as it were Israel voting against. Article 4 was questionable since it appeared to acknowledge the idea of "just wars." Convention 2 (Convention Extra to the Geneva Traditions of 12 Admirable 1949 and Relating to the Security of Casualties of Non-International Clashes), grows securities concerning therapeutic work force, legal ensures, and human treatment. An address approximately Convention II has been what level of struggle triggers its application.

One of the questions in the twenty-first century was to what degree the law of war applies to non-state on-screen characters, as in the past it had for the most part been pertinent to clashes between states. Regarding those confined at Guantanamo Cove, Cuba, and the Bush Organization claimed that the Geneva Traditions assurances did not apply, fundamentally since those held there were assigned as unlawful adversary combatants. Lawyers like John Yoo contended for a modern worldview of illicit foe combatants since psychological militants, on his see, were not one or the other warriors nor civilians. Agreeing to a Presidential reminder (7 February 2002), the Geneva Traditions did not apply to the strife with Al-

Qaeda and in spite of the fact that they connected to the strife in Afghanistan, the Taliban were treated as illegal combatants. As illicit foe combatants, that is, people who do not wear regalia or carry their arms straightforwardly, they did not have the status of being detainees of war, and may not advantage from the securities ensured by the Geneva Traditions, such as not being subject to indictment for murdering. The US government too depended on reservations to key settlements as a reason for denying assurance to the prisoners, indeed in spite of the fact that a few considered them invalid reservations since they were conflicting with the protest and reason of the settlements. Besides, the US government contended that since they were held exterior the US, they were too not entitled to intrinsically ensure due handle protections.

While a few contend that the war on fear is not one or the other an equipped struggle between states nor a struggle of a non-international character, others fought that the conventional law of war may be connected to psychological militants without huge trouble. Indeed, civilians get securities beneath the Fourth Geneva Tradition and the Common Article Three. Thus, those held in Guantanamo ought to have gotten at the exceptionally slightest, the rights ensured to civilians, which incorporate the right to a hearing some time recently a officer and compassionate treatment. In brief, the prevailing see in worldwide law was that the Common Article Three was expecting to give at slightest a essential least of security in circumstances of strife that did not something else fit the scope of scope given by the Geneva Traditions. Concurring to this rationale, adversary combatants ought to advantage from the securities managed civilians beneath the Common Article Three.

The US Preeminent Court bargains with questions approximately the degree to which universal law and sacred standards are connected to the prisoners in a set of three of cases. The to begin with detainees were taken to Guantanamo Narrows, Cuba, 11 January 2002. Although the Bush Organization did not discharge measurements around the number held, a few hundred people from over 44 nations are accepted to have been held there in uncertain detainment. They were in a legitimate limbo, as the US government did not record charges against them; 5 a long time afterward charges were as it were recorded against ten prisoners. Most were held for over a year in lamentable conditions, and they were not permitted contact with their families or attorneys.

The Center for Protected Rights took the lead in recording suits on sake of the prisoners. On 28 June 2004, the US Preeminent Court vindicated their rights. In Rasul v. Bush the Court held that those held on Guantanamo Inlet, Cuba was entitled to challenge the lawfulness of their detainment. In Hamdi v. Rumsfeld the Court concluded that prisoners were entitled to challenge the legitimateness of their detainment in habeas corpus procedures. Rumsfeld v. Padilla was rejected on procedural grounds (the case ought to have been recorded in South Carolina where Padilla was held or maybe than Modern York). The in general result was a awesome triumph, as the US Incomparable Court rejected the idea that the prisoners were without legitimate response and ruled that they seem challenge their detainment in court. As Jonathan Hafetz persuasively states: "The broader standards supporting these cases recommend that not one or the other citizenship nor the put of detainment can conclusively decide the scope of accessible lawful protections." This fortifies the center thought of human rights, that they are not unexpected on nationality, topographical area, or any other attribute.

In reaction to the choices the US government set up Combatant Status Audit Tribunals to choose if prisoners were adversary combatants. On 30 December 2005, President Bush marked into law the Prisoner Treatment Act. In Hamdan v. Rumsfeld, the Court said the military commissions damaged US and universal law. The Common Article Three of the Geneva Traditions did apply to Guantanamo prisoners. The case included the address of whether the President had surpassed his specialist by building up the commissions without the back of Congress. To correct that, Congress at that point passed the Military Commissions Act (MCA) which Bush marked into law on 17 October 2006. As it endeavored to constrain habeas corpus procedures encourage, claims were recorded challenging the proceeding refusal of habeas corpus and the legitimacy of the MCA of 2006.

A few individuals of Congress oppose this idea with the Bush Organization. For occurrence, Congressperson Tom Harkin, a Democrat from Iowa, who presented a charge to near the Guantanmo Inlet detainment office in June 2007.

Human Rights amid Gracious Conflict: Derogations

When there is residential turmoil and the law of war does not apply, the worldwide law of human rights concerning states of crisis is utilized. Beneath these circumstances states will claim that they must suspend or 'derogate from' worldwide human rights guidelines. Article 4 of the ICCPR, concerning the issue of when a open crisis undermines the life of the country, licenses discrediting for a few human rights, but not for principal ones such as the right to life, the right against genocide, the right against torment, the right against servitude, and the right against subjective capture and detainment. Article 15 of the European Tradition on Human Rights moreover permits for criticisms "to the degree entirely required by the exigencies of the situation" in the case of open crisis or in time of war. The American Tradition on Human Rights contains Article 27, Suspension of Ensures, which grants criticism "in time of war, open threat, or other crisis that undermines the autonomy or security of a State Party." Whereas its detailing appears to give the most effortless implies of defending criticism, the drafting history (travaux preparatory) recommends otherwise.

All three settlements incorporate the key concept of proportionality, allowing disparagements as it were to the degree "strictly required by the exigencies of the situation." All three too require formal notice of specialists who can screen the usage of the criticism approaches. Where they contrast is in the rights that they characterize as outright rights that can never be suspended, that is, non-dirigible rights.

In Eminent 2001 the Human Rights Committee issued a Common Comment on Article 4 of the ICCPR indicating the vital limits on disparagements in a majority rule society. It was momentous that it dispersed the approach days some time recently the awful 9/11 assaults. One of its most critical focuses is that certain rights can never be suspended, no matter what sort of open crisis a state face. One of these is the forbiddance against torment or pitiless, barbaric, or debasing treatment or discipline. The challenges to human rights approaches such as this one in the twenty-first century will include counterterrorism arrangements embraced in the repercussions of the appalling occasions related with 11 September.

The Worldwide Criminal Court

There has long been a require for a worldwide court with the specialist to uphold worldwide human rights law and helpful law. For decades there were recommendations on the table to build up a changeless universal criminal court that would have the control to rebuff those capable for the most noticeably awful outrages. In the repercussions of the genocides in the previous Yugoslavia and in Rwanda when the universal community set up advertisement hoc tribunals to address the outrages committed in these extraordinary areas, a seen require having a changeless institution to arraign violators of these standards driven to reestablished endeavors to build up such a tribunal. The contentions for its creation incorporate: hindering future outrages, dodging the struggle of intrigued inalienable in household court martials, and deterring the require seizing respondents to put them on trial, as in the Eichman and Alvarez-Machain cases, or to go through the awkward handle of removal, as in the Soering case. In July 1998 a preliminary conference met in Rome to finalize a statute for the proposed lasting worldwide tribunal. One hundred and twenty states voted to favor the last archive, and the Worldwide Criminal Court (ICC) was set up in July 2002, a month after 60 states confirmed the treaty.

Article 5 of the Rome Statute of the ICC records four categories of violations which drop beneath the Court's purview: genocide, wrongdoings against humankind, war violations, and hostility. Circumstances can be alluded to the ICC by states parties, the prosecutor, or the Security Committee. As it does not have retroactive purview, it can as it were listened to things that happen after the point in time that the Rome Statute came into impact, that is,

1 July 2002. The ICC works concurring to the rule of complementarity, which implies that it can arraign people if the state with ward over the matter is unwilling or incapable to do so.

Although the completion of the Statute was a triumph, human rights advocates had a few genuine reactions. To begin with, the purview of the tribunal remained vague since the conference did not decipher a few of the violations. Although violations of animosity show up in the Statute, they are not characterized. A concession to Security Board individuals using atomic control come about in characterizing war violations so that they did not incorporate any reference to atomic weapons. In expansion, landmines were avoided from the Statute, due to restriction by the Joined together States, Russia, China, and Britain. Although the Statute notices "enforced vanishings of persons" as a wrongdoing against humankind, there was a terrible stipulation that the vanishings may be indicted as it were if they happen for a "prolonged period of time."

Another discussion spun around the child warrior arrangements. Article 8(2)(e) vii of the Statute holds that it is a war wrongdoing to recruit or enroll children beneath the age of 15 in outfitted powers or bunches or to utilize them in outfitted strife, although most human rights activists contended unequivocally for raising the age constrain to 18. The Joined together States driven the campaign to lower the age to 15 since of its hone of selecting 17-year-olds. Despite the 15-year run the show, the Statute indicates that the ICC will not have ward over children who were beneath 18 at the time of the affirmed commission of violations (Article 26).

Another major feedback is that the Statute acknowledges the defense of prevalent orders in Article

33, although this defense has never been recognized in worldwide law and was rejected at the Nuremberg and Tokyo tribunals. The basis for the defense is that warriors ought to not be held mindful for violations committed when they are taking after the orders of their predominant officers.

A potential disparity may result since the universal tribunal, like the Yugoslav and Rwandan tribunals, will not have the control to force the passing punishment, indeed although residential courts may use this control. Thus, the more senior authorities, if arraigned in the worldwide criminal court, will confront less serious discipline than would junior officers attempted in national courts.

It is critical that there were prior endeavors to define a code of universal wrongdoings. Propelled by the Nuremberg standards, the ILC worked on a Draft Code of Wrongdoings against the Peace and Security of Mankind. In 1954 the ILC sent the report to the UN Common Gathering, which took 27 a long time some time recently sending it back to the ILC for elaboration. Another adaptation was wrapped up in 1991. It applies as it were to people, and not to states. A partitioned instrument, the Draft Articles on State Duty, incorporates a arrangement showing that the arraignment of people for wrongdoings against the peace and security of mankind does not calm the state of obligation beneath universal law.

Although the ICC has as it have been in operation a few a long time, four circumstances have been alluded to the Prosecutor. Three were submitted by states parties around issues inside their borders. The Security Chamber alluded the circumstance in Darfur since Sudan is not a party to the Rome Statute. After undertaking a few inquire about, the Prosecutor started to examine three of them – in Uganda, the Law based Republic of the Congo, and Darfur, Sudan. In July 2005 the office started to issue capture warrants.

The ICC is considered a momentous accomplishment in the universal community. One development was counting sexual savagery in the definition of violations against humankind in Article 7(1)(g). The Statute records different shapes of sexual viciousness as violations against humankind: assault, sexual subjugation, implemented prostitution, constrained pregnancy, implemented sterilization, or any other shape of sexual viciousness of comparable gravity. The term "forced pregnancy" was included although antiabortionists communicated concern that this state would infer bolster for lawful fetus removal. Blunt rivals included the Vatican, Ireland, and antiabortion NGOs. The Statute in Article 7(2)(f) says that the definition of constrained pregnancy might not in any way be translated as influencing national laws relating to pregnancy. Consideration of the state was considered a critical triumph since the hone of constrained pregnancy was a key technique in 'ethnic cleansing' arrangements in the previous Yugoslavia; troopers purposely assaulted ladies of the adversary ethnic gather, driving them to carry the pregnancies to term. The thought was to alter the ethnic composition of the populace (as the child had the father's character). Ladies were rejected by their spouses and communities; they either rejected the descendant or in interviews said they would raise them to strike back against their fathers. Universal attorneys too demanded that assault be recognized as a war wrongdoing. Although the advertisement hoc worldwide criminal tribunals for Yugoslavia and Rwanda were to some degree reluctant to do so, assault is considered a war wrongdoing in the statute of the ICC.

Another development was permitting casualties to take an interest in the lawful procedures and to get reparations. The ICC is moreover anticipated to build up a believe finance for casualties of abominations.

CHAPTER VI

FUNCTIONING OF NATIONAL AND INTERNATIONAL NGOs

Any discussion of the provision of aid through civil society organizations (CSOs) needs to consider the case of international non-governmental organizations (INGOs). They are a powerful force in the delivery of aid, and important actors within the international development architecture. They are now providing more aid to developing countries than ever before, and the budgets of particularly large INGOs have surpassed those of some Organisation for Economic Co-operation and Development (OECD) donor countries. Eight INGOs (World Vision International, Oxfam International, Save the Children International, Plan International, Médecins Sans Frontières, CARE International, CARITAS International and ActionAid International) had combined revenue of more than US$11.7 billion in 2011, up 40 percent since 2005. INGOs represent a major presence in many developing countries, receive substantial sums from donors to carry out humanitarian assistance and development work, and are an increasingly influential actor in policy processes and in the global governance of aid. Non-governmental organizations (NGOs) are non-profit organizations that work to improve the lives of people in need. They can operate at the local, national, or international level, and their functions include:

- **Providing services**: NGOs can provide essential goods and services to people affected by natural disasters or other challenges.

- **Advocating for change:** NGOs can advocate for policies and practices that benefit disadvantaged communities.
- **Mobilizing resources:** NGOs can mobilize financial and human resources to ensure that aid is delivered effectively and in a timely manner.
- **Partnering with other organizations:** NGOs can work with other organizations, including government agencies, to address complex challenges.
- **Connecting with communities:** NGOs can work at the grassroots level to connect with communities directly and tailor their services to meet specific needs.
- **Supporting infrastructure:** Some NGOs focus on supporting infrastructure development and maintenance, such as building schools, hospitals, wells, and public restrooms.

Nature of INGOs - What distinguishes INGOs from National CSOs in Both Donor Countries and Host Countries?

INGOs in donor countries are different from other national CSOs in donor and recipient countries in several respects, including in terms of their global operations, their size, and scale, and geographic reach, access to funds, budgets, and roles in development. Membership of global consortia: A key factor that distinguishes INGOS from national CSOs in donor countries is that they have global operations. INGOs usually have multiple autonomous national offices based in many OECD and some middle-income developing countries, but they also operate together as members of global consortia, confederations or affiliations that undertake development programmes through their own regional and national offices in many developing countries. Thus Oxfam Canada, for instance, is an autonomous organization with its own governance structure but is a member of the Oxfam International confederation that has 16 other member organizations. CARE USA is a member of CARE International, a confederation of 14 member organizations. Global reach: INGOs have extensive global programmatic reach as a result of their membership of global confederations. While individual national INGO affiliates may only directly manage or operate programmes in a relatively small number of countries, they can participate across the whole range of the confederation's programme countries (by providing financial resources or advice). For instance, Save the Children works in 120 countries globally, 3 World Vision International in 98 countries, 4 and Oxfam International in more than 90 countries. 5 The global reach of INGOs often exceeds that of many individual OECD official donor bilateral geographic programmes. Size and scope: INGOs are generally much larger than other national CSOs in donor countries, in terms of budgets, number of staff, and operations. For instance, in Australia, two of the main INGOs (Oxfam Australia and World Vision Australia) have over 200 members of staff based in Australia, whereas nearly all other national CSOs have under 50, and usually much fewer. INGOs also typically have much larger budgets than national CSOs: in 2011 World Vision Australia's revenue was US$345 million,6 and Oxfam Australia's was US$76.5 million, compared to most national CSOs that had revenue below US$10 million, and many of them below US$1 million. The much larger budgets that INGOs command is the result of a range of factors, including increased capacity for fundraising from the public, governments and other institutions, greater legitimacy and influence with government and other donors, and greater capacity to use funds at economies of scale.

These factors also mean that large INGOs are more likely to gain core or framework funding agreements from donor governments, and in larger amounts. National level INGOs are also able to tap into the global financial and staff resources of their confederations (discussed more in Section 3). Organizational capacity: INGOs' larger budgets and staff contingents allow for dedicated staff across a full range of operations and programming, meaning that INGOs generally have both broader and deeper capacity than national CSOs. INGOs typically have.

An Overview of International NGOs in Development (often in dedicated teams) undertaking roles in organizational management, development programme implementation and management, humanitarian assistance, fundraising, communications and media, human resource management, finance and accounting, and policy and campaigning. Individual INGO national affiliates can also draw on the staff resources and expertise of their confederation members. In comparison, staff of national CSOs are often responsible for several roles in the organization or make strategic decisions on where to concentrate staff resources (for instance, on how much staff time to dedicate to managing existing development programmes versus developing new programmes). Many INGOs now also have dedicated staff working on monitoring, evaluation, and learning. This allows INGOs to assess the results and impact of their work, to implement quality assurance and improvement measures, demonstrate accountability to partners, recipients, and the public, and to report efficiently to donors on how funds have been used and on the overall impact of funded programmes. This type of work is specialized, resource-intensive and time consuming, and many smaller national CSOs have limited capacity to undertake it, concentrating most of their efforts in reporting to official donors and their fundraising publics. Range of partnerships: While most national CSOs in donor countries adopt a partnership approach to development programming, INGOs often work across a broader range of partnerships, and have the advantage that they can bring to these partnerships greater financial and other resources (in particular, expertise and knowledge). Like national CSOs, INGOs typically work in partnership with developing-country CSOs. However, their partnerships in both donor and developing countries increasingly also extend to other institutions and the private sector.

They are increasingly collaborating with academic and research centres, as well as the private sector, in the design and delivery of programmes, and drawing on additional resources from their consortium members when they do so. In some cases, INGOs will also partner or collaborate with other INGOs, but are less likely to do so with national donor-country CSOs. Legitimacy and influence: INGOs' size and scale, global reach, large staff contingents, range of programmes and partnerships and ability to demonstrate results afford them a level of professionalism, credibility, and legitimacy in the eyes of donors and the public. As a result, INGOs have a comparatively higher profile than national CSOs, both with the public and with government and other donors. Although governments require INGOs to meet stringent eligibility and accountability requirements, they generally regard the largest INGOs as established development actors that have proven track records and, therefore, as trustworthy channels for the delivery of aid. In comparison, while seen as legitimate, national CSOs sometimes have a more difficult time demonstrating their eligibility for funding, because they do not have comparable levels of programme scale, staff capacity and resources. Greater visibility and reputation also allow INGOs to maintain their advantageous positions: they are better placed and can draw on greater resources to continue to demonstrate their legitimacy and to undertake continued fundraising. These factors also mean that INGOs can have greater standing and 'voice' with decision makers, funding agencies and within policy processes. INGOs are, therefore, generally in a position to influence more strongly both the domestic and international.

What are the Roles of INGOs in International Development Cooperation?

INGO mission and mandate: INGOs have varied roles in development cooperation and have varied approaches based on different models of development practice. However, there are strong similarities in the objectives they aim to achieve, and in their overall mandates. Key objectives for INGOs typically include the reduction of poverty and inequality, the realization of rights, the promotion of gender equality and social justice, protection of the environment and strengthening of civil society and democratic governance. For example, three of the largest INGOs have primary objectives based on poverty reduction:

- CARE International "shares a common vision to fight against worldwide poverty and to protect and enhance human dignity."
- Oxfam International is a "global movement for change, to build a future free from the injustice of poverty."

- World Vision is "dedicated to working with children, families and communities to overcome poverty and injustice."

INGO target groups and sectors: INGOs work with a wide range of target groups and sectors to achieve their development objectives. While some have a special focus, many work in similar areas. Save The Children and Plan International, as their names suggest, have a specific focus on children and undertake programmes in health, nutrition, education, protection, and child rights. ActionAid works on food rights, women's rights, democratic governance, education, climate change and HIV/AIDS.12 Many INGOs, such as World Vision International or Oxfam International, are involved in humanitarian assistance as well as long term development programmes.

One of the world's largest INGOs, Médecins sans Frontières works only on humanitarian assistance, delivering emergency aid "to people affected by armed conflict, epidemics, healthcare exclusion and natural or man-made disasters". Programme approaches: Most INGOs are directly involved in planning, implementing and managing development programmes and humanitarian assistance in developing countries. Their approaches can range from the operational implementation of programmes, to working wholly through partners, where they have no direct role in programme implementation. Most INGOs undertake a mix of approaches, often informed by practice models and theoretical frameworks, and by performance and quality standards. In these respects, INGOs do not necessarily differ from national CSOs: the difference, as stated above, relates to the scale and geographic reach of INGOs' programmatic approaches.

Policy dialogue and campaigning: Some INGOs are also involved in policy dialogue, advocacy, lobbying and campaigning work at the domestic and international level. This work may be undertaken as part of global campaigns or coalitions and is usually designed to bring about structural or policy change.

An Overview of International NGOs in Development Cooperation in relation to development problems

These roles are connected to a view that, in addition to undertaking programmes in developing countries to address the symptoms of poverty, CSOs should also be involved in addressing the underlying causes of poverty — and that this means undertaking policy dialogue and influencing roles. As a result, INGOs such as World Vision and CARE have increased their policy, advocacy and campaigning roles in recent years. For instance, CARE states that:

"Advocacy is a key aspect of CARE's humanitarian and development efforts, addressing not only the immediate needs of the poor, but also the root causes of poverty and obstacles to its elimination."

Increasing role in research: INGOs draw on the global reach and the cumulative experience of their confederation members for both their programme delivery and for their policy influence work. They undertake research and learning processes to ensure that both their development programmes and their policy influence work are informed by their own programme experience and knowledge, and by their relationships with developing country partners and communities. Increasingly, some INGOs are commissioning research to establish a stronger evidence base for both programming and policy influence. Many national INGO affiliates now have dedicated research units, along with teams in the international secretariat of INGOs (their consortium's coordinating body). For instance, in the first half of 2012, the Oxfam International research unit produced reports on climate change, food security, the arms trade and the African Union. Changing roles for a changing world: Like official donors and other international development institutions, INGO roles are not static: they change and respond to the changing global context for development. Some commentators suggest that changing geopolitical dynamics at the global level have implications for the roles of INGOs. In this context, INGOs are assuming greater and more important roles at the supranational level, ensuring that global public goods are handled and distributed in ways that benefit rather than disadvantage poor people. INGOs are also increasingly drawing on their capacity to work with States and international organizations to address transnational problems, such as climate change, global poverty, urbanization, complex humanitarian crises and security threats in a globalized world.

CHAPTER VII

A TESTAMENT TO HUMANITY: NGOs IN WAR-TORN REGIONS

Outstanding and Commendable work done by Local and International NGOs in war hit areas for rescue and aid of affected people – An Overview

A Testament to Humanity

Non-Governmental Organizations (NGOs) have consistently proven to be a lifeline for countless individuals affected by war and conflict. Their tireless efforts in providing aid, protection, and support have made a significant impact on the lives of millions. While NGOs face numerous challenges, including security risks, access restrictions, and funding shortages, their unwavering commitment to helping those in need continues to inspire hope. They serve as a beacon of hope, providing critical assistance and advocating for justice in the darkest of times.

Collaboration is essential when seeking solutions to complex problems. This is the case for natural disasters, where the effects are so vast that no one entity or organization can solve every problem and assist every person in need of help. Collaboration, cooperation, communication, and coordination are all words that tend to get used interchangeably when referring to two or more groups working together.

However, collaboration stands apart from the others as it is not simply about working together, but rather creating something new and better because of that shared work (Denise, 1999). Collaboration contains elements of cooperation, communication, and coordination in order to be achieved, but collaboration is what is truly integral to successful disaster relief. Collaboration can be defined as "the process of shared creation: two or more individuals with complementary skills interacting to create a shared understanding that none had previously possessed or could have come to on their own" (Schrage, 1990, p. 140). Though this term is frequently used in a variety of settings it holds significant importance to the implementation of real and meaningful solutions to the problems created by natural disasters and their devastating effects on humanity around the world. We will return to the topic of collaboration and coordination after discussing disaster response, the role of international politics, NGOs, and organizational learning.

The Indispensable Role of NGOs

In the face of war and conflict, Non-Governmental Organizations (NGOs) have consistently demonstrated their commitment to alleviating human suffering. These organizations, both local and international, have been instrumental in providing critical aid and support to millions of people affected by war.

Responding to Disaster Natural disasters are unavoidable and horrendous events in numerous ways including loss of life, hindering country's ability to function, and high costs of rebuilding and providing relief after they occur. As Comfort, Ko and Zagorecki highlight in their 2004 study, not only do disasters create physical problems (such as injuries and infrastructure damage), but they also 8 damage "sociocultural infrastructure," meaning economic, social, and organizational components of communities. This makes disasters a multifaceted problem for nations to prepare for, deal with, and overcome afterwards. Sadly, according to studies it seems that natural disasters are not only here to stay, but are actually getting worse (Von Medling, Oyedele, Cleland, Spillane & Konanahalli, 2011; Mannakkara & Wilkinson, 2013). These studies point out that climate change appears to be making storms and disasters both more frequent and intense than before. This demonstrates how vital it is for organizations, nations, and governments to have adequate responses to these disasters. There are four phases of the disaster cycle that have been identified - mitigation and preparedness (which occur beforehand), response (during and after), and recovery (short and long-term actions following the disaster) (Von Medling et al., 2011). While mitigation and preparedness are vital to a community's outcome following a natural disaster, there is ultimately no way to stop these disasters, only minimize the damage they have done and help as much as possible in the aftermath. All phases are important to the process, but this study will focus primarily on the response and recovery phases.

According to Comfort, Ko and Zagorecki's study in 2004, the initial stages of response involve protecting lives and helping the injured, while the recovery periods focus on long-term effects, such as unemployment, infrastructure, medical care and housing. Proper response upfront can significantly lessen the needs during recovery in the long-term. Disaster relief includes a variety of activities to help assist communities that have been affected by natural disasters. Tierney, Lindell, and Perry defined disaster relief as activities that "reduce physical, social, and economic vulnerability and to facilitate the effective provision of short-term emergency assistance and longer-term recovery aid" (2001, p. 256). Generally, this 9 equates to improving life and can include actions such as rebuilding, mitigation efforts, repairs, regulations, and other activities that aim to better the current state of things and improve (Von Meding et al., 2011). There are various methods for disaster relief, and many have different ideas as to what is the best way to really help. The "Build Back Better" strategy proposed by Bill Clinton following the tsunami in East Asia offers a holistic approach to recovery that tries not only to restore communities but improve them and make them more resilient (Mannakkara & Wilkinson, 2013). Other studies have emphasized the need for information to determine "demand flow," using estimates of magnitude and effect to figure out how much help and supplies are needed (Comfort et al., 2004). These sorts of strategies rely on multiple partners effectively working together to share information or create a fully holistic approach to relief.

There has not been a consensus on the most effective strategy for response and recovery, but almost all strategies incorporate collaboration as a necessity to success. Natural disasters are often too vast and harmful for one entity to fix everything on their own, which is why collaboration becomes so necessary in assisting in these dire and crucial moments. According to Hutchinton's study, earthquakes specifically, which will be the primary focus on this study, provoke two responses from the international community: either they are overwhelmed by the devastation and believe the high price of repair and aid make intervention impossible, or they see international organization as the only way to help (2000). Walking away from those in need would be a mistake by the international community, so the only way to overcome these devastating tragedies is to join. "Large and seemingly unsolvable problems are best approached from a cooperative angle, combing resources and preventing duplication" (Kapucu, 2008, p. 256).

Kapucu highlights here that there is no better way to 10 overcome a daunting task, such as disaster relief, than systematically working to share resources and delegate tasks.

Key Contributions of NGOs

Emergency Relief: National and international NGOs play a crucial role in providing critical medical aid to individuals affected by war and conflict.

Key Roles of NGOs in Medical Aid

- **Emergency Medical Care:**

  - **Field Hospitals:** Setting up temporary medical facilities to provide immediate care for injuries and illnesses.
  - **Mobile Clinics:** Deploying mobile clinics to reach remote and inaccessible areas.
  - **Surgical Interventions:** Performing life-saving surgeries, including trauma surgery, orthopedic surgery, and emergency cesarean sections.

- **Disease Prevention and Control:**

  - **Vaccination Campaigns:** Implementing vaccination programs to prevent outbreaks of infectious diseases.
  - **Malnutrition Treatment:** Providing therapeutic food to treat malnourished children and adults.
  - **Hygiene Promotion:** Educating communities about hygiene practices to reduce the spread of diseases.

- **Mental Health Support:**

- **Counseling Services:** Offering psychological counseling to individuals and families affected by trauma.
- **Stress Management Techniques:** Teaching coping mechanisms to help people deal with the emotional impact of war.

• **Medical Supply Distribution:**

- **Essential Medications:** Providing essential medicines, including antibiotics, pain relievers, and vaccines.
- **Medical Equipment:** Distributing medical equipment, such as surgical instruments, diagnostic tools, and hospital beds.

Notable International NGOs Providing Medical Aid

• **Doctors Without Borders (MSF):** Renowned for its work in conflict zones, MSF provides emergency medical aid, including surgery, maternal healthcare, and treatment for infectious diseases.
• **International Committee of the Red Cross (ICRC):** Offers a wide range of medical services, including first aid, emergency surgery, and rehabilitation.
• **World Health Organization (WHO):** Coordinates international efforts to improve global health, including responding to health crises in war-torn regions.

Challenges Faced by NGOs

• **Security Risks:** Operating in conflict zones exposes medical personnel to danger from armed groups, landmines, and other threats.

- **Access Restrictions:** Governments or armed groups may limit access to affected populations, hindering the delivery of aid.
- **Funding Shortages:** The increasing number of conflicts and humanitarian crises can strain resources.
- **Complex Political and Social Environments:** Navigating the complexities of local politics and cultural sensitivities can be difficult.

Despite these challenges, NGOs continue to play a vital role in saving lives and alleviating suffering in war-torn regions. Their dedication and commitment to providing medical aid in the face of adversity are truly inspiring. The organizations work tirelessly to deliver essential healthcare services, even in the most challenging circumstances. Providing immediate medical care, setting up field hospitals, and distributing essential medicines.

Food and Water as a Support by National and International NGOs

Delivering food and water to displaced populations and those trapped in conflict zones. Food and Water Support by NGOs in War Zones in war-torn regions, access to food and water often becomes a critical lifeline for millions of people. NGOs play a pivotal role in providing these essential resources, helping to sustain life and mitigate suffering.

Key strategies employed by NGOs to address food and water needs in war zones:

Food Distribution

- **Emergency Food Aid:** Providing immediate food assistance, such as ready-to-eat meals, to individuals and families displaced by conflict.

- **Food Security Programs:** Implementing long-term programs to improve food security, including agricultural training, seed distribution, and support for local food production.
- **Nutrition Support:** Providing supplementary and therapeutic food to address malnutrition, particularly in children and pregnant women.
- **Food Vouchers:** Distributing food vouchers to enable people to purchase food from local markets, stimulating the local economy.

Water Supply and Sanitation

- **Water Treatment and Distribution:** Providing safe drinking water through water treatment plants, water purification tablets, and water distribution systems.
- **Sanitation Facilities:** Constructing and maintaining latrines and sanitation facilities to prevent the spread of waterborne diseases.
- **Hygiene Promotion:** Educating communities about proper hygiene practices, including handwashing and sanitation.

Notable NGOs Involved in Food and Water Aid

- **World Food Programme (WFP):** The world's largest humanitarian organization, WFP provides food assistance to millions of people affected by conflict and disasters.
- **Oxfam:** This global confederation works to overcome poverty and inequality, including providing food aid and water sanitation services in war zones.

- **CARE International:** This humanitarian organization focuses on fighting poverty and social injustice, delivering food and water assistance to vulnerable populations.
- **International Committee of the Red Cross (ICRC):** The ICRC provides essential humanitarian aid, including food and water, to people affected by armed conflict.
- **Doctors Without Borders (MSF):** In addition to medical aid, MSF often provides food and water to people in crisis-affected areas.

It's important to note that NGOs often face significant challenges in delivering food and water aid in war zones, including security risks, access restrictions, and logistical hurdles. Despite these challenges, they remain committed to providing life-saving assistance to those in need.

Shelter as a Support by National and International NGOs

Constructing temporary shelters and providing blankets, mattresses, and other essential items. In the face of war and conflict, millions of people are displaced from their homes, often forced to seek refuge in makeshift shelters or overcrowded camps. NGOs play a critical role in providing emergency shelter and supporting long-term housing solutions.

Key areas of shelter support provided by NGOs:
Emergency Shelter

- **Tents and Tarpaulins:** Distributing tents, tarpaulins, and other temporary shelter materials to provide immediate protection from the elements.
- **Evacuation and Relocation:** Assisting in the evacuation of people from dangerous areas and providing

temporary shelter in safer locations.

- **Non-Food Items (NFIs):** Providing essential items such as blankets, sleeping bags, and cooking utensils to help people survive in harsh conditions.

Transitional Shelter

- **Collective Shelters:** Establishing and managing collective shelters, such as camps and communal housing, for displaced populations.
- **Rental Subsidies:** Providing financial assistance to help people rent temporary housing.
- **Housing Repair Kits:** Distributing repair kits and tools to help people repair damaged homes.

Permanent Housing Solutions

- **Reconstruction and Rehabilitation:** Supporting the reconstruction of homes and infrastructure damaged by conflict.
- **Housing Grants:** Providing financial assistance to help people rebuild their homes.
- **Land Tenure Security:** Assisting in securing land rights to ensure long-term housing stability.

Notable NGOs Involved in Shelter Support

- **International Committee of the Red Cross (ICRC):** The ICRC provides emergency shelter, including tents, blankets, and other essential items, to people affected by conflict.
- **UNHCR, the UN Refugee Agency:** UNHCR works to protect refugees and internally displaced persons,

providing emergency shelter and supporting long-term housing solutions.

- **Oxfam:** Oxfam provides shelter and housing solutions, including the construction of temporary shelters and the rehabilitation of damaged homes.
- **CARE International:** CARE provides emergency shelter, including tents, blankets, and other essential items, as well as long-term housing solutions.
- **Save the Children:** Save the Children provides emergency shelter and support to children and families affected by conflict.

By providing essential shelter and housing solutions, NGOs help to protect vulnerable populations, restore a sense of normalcy, and contribute to the overall recovery process in war-torn regions.

- **Protection of Civilians:**

  - **Advocacy:** Lobbying for the protection of civilians and holding accountable those who violate international humanitarian law.
  - **Human Rights Monitoring:** Documenting human rights abuses and advocating for justice.

- **Long-Term Recovery and Reconstruction:**

  - **Education:** Supporting education initiatives, rebuilding schools, and providing educational materials.
  - **Economic Recovery:** Providing microfinance loans and job training to help people rebuild their lives.

- ○ **Psychological Support:** Offering counseling and mental health services to individuals and communities affected by trauma.

Notable NGOs and Their Impact:

- **International Committee of the Red Cross (ICRC):** A neutral and impartial organization that provides humanitarian assistance to victims of armed conflict and other violence.
- **Doctors Without Borders (MSF):** A medical humanitarian organization that provides emergency medical aid to people affected by conflict, epidemics, and natural disasters.
- **Save the Children:** A global organization that works to save children's lives, fight for their rights, and help them fulfil their potential.
- **CARE International:** A global humanitarian organization that fights poverty and social injustice.
- **Oxfam:** A global confederation of 21 independent charitable organizations focusing on the alleviation of global poverty.

The Challenge of Operating in War Zones

NGOs often face significant challenges while operating in war-torn regions, including:

- **Security Risks:** Staff members may be targeted by armed groups or face threats from other actors.
- **Direct Threats:** NGO staff, particularly those working in frontline areas, are often targets for attacks, kidnappings, and violence.

- **Landmines and Explosive Remnants of War (ERW):** These pose a serious threat to aid workers and the communities they serve.
- **Armed Groups:** Navigating complex political landscapes and dealing with armed groups can be challenging and risky.
- **Access Restrictions:** Governments or armed groups may restrict access to affected populations.
- **Government Restrictions:** Governments may impose restrictions on the movement of aid workers and the delivery of aid, hindering humanitarian efforts.
- **Conflict Zones:** Access to conflict zones can be limited due to active fighting, making it difficult to reach people in need.
- **Bureaucratic Hurdles:** Complex bureaucratic procedures and red tape can delay the delivery of aid.
- **Funding Shortages:** The increasing number of conflicts and humanitarian crises can strain resources.
- **Complex Political and Social Environments:** Navigating the complexities of local politics and cultural sensitivities can be difficult.

Funding Shortages to National and International NGOs

- **Competing Needs:** The increasing number of humanitarian crises worldwide can lead to competition for limited funding.
- **Donor Fatigue:** Donors may become less willing to contribute to long-term humanitarian efforts.
- **Economic Downturns:** Economic downturns can reduce the amount of funding available for humanitarian aid.

Logistical Challenges to National and International NGOs

Infrastructure Damage Challenges: War often damages infrastructure, making it difficult to transport aid supplies. NGOs often operate in challenging environments, especially during emergencies. While their primary focus is on providing aid and support to affected populations, they can also face significant infrastructural damages that hinder their operations.

Physical Infrastructure Damage:

- **Office Buildings and Warehouses:** Damage to offices, warehouses, and storage facilities can disrupt operations, leading to loss of equipment, supplies, and important documents.
- **Vehicles and Equipment:** Damage to vehicles, generators, and other equipment can hinder transportation and the delivery of aid.
- **Communication Systems:** Damage to communication systems, such as phones, radios, and internet connections, can disrupt coordination and information sharing.

Human Resource Challenges:

- **Staff Safety:** The safety of NGO staff can be compromised due to security threats, natural disasters, or accidents.
- **Staff Morale:** The demanding nature of emergency response can lead to burnout and decreased morale among staff.
- **Staff Turnover:** High turnover rates can impact the organization's capacity to respond effectively.

Financial Implications:

- **Increased Costs:** Repairing damaged infrastructure and replacing lost equipment can incur significant costs.
- **Reduced Funding:** Emergency responses can deplete an NGO's financial resources, affecting future operations.
- **Insurance Claims:** Processing insurance claims can be time-consuming and may not fully cover the losses.

Operational Challenges:

- **Supply Chain Disruptions:** Damage to infrastructure can disrupt the supply chain, leading to delays in the delivery of aid.
- **Security Risks:** Increased security threats can make it difficult to operate safely and efficiently.
- **Logistical Challenges:** Damage to roads, bridges, and other infrastructure can hinder transportation and distribution of aid.

Supply Chain Disruptions to National and International NGOs

Supply chain disruptions pose significant challenges to both national and international NGOs. These disruptions can hinder their ability to deliver essential aid and services, impacting their operations and ultimately the people they serve.

Here are some of the key supply chain disruptions that affect NGOs:

Global Supply Chain Disruptions

- **Pandemics:** Global health crises like COVID-19 have disrupted supply chains, leading to shortages of essential medical supplies, food, and other goods.

- **Geopolitical Tensions:** Trade wars, political instability, and geopolitical conflicts can disrupt global supply chains, affecting the availability and cost of goods.
- **Natural Disasters:** Natural disasters such as earthquakes, floods, and hurricanes can damage infrastructure and disrupt transportation networks, hindering the movement of goods.

Local Supply Chain Disruptions

- **Conflict and Instability:** War and conflict can damage infrastructure, disrupt transportation networks, and limit access to resources.
- **Security Risks:** Security threats, such as terrorism and piracy, can make it difficult to transport goods safely.
- **Corruption and Inefficiency:** Corruption and bureaucratic hurdles can slow down the movement of goods and increase costs.

Impact on NGO Operations

- **Delayed Aid Delivery:** Disruptions can delay the delivery of essential aid, such as food, medicine, and shelter materials.
- **Increased Costs:** Supply chain disruptions can lead to higher costs for transportation, logistics, and procurement.
- **Reduced Effectiveness:** Limited access to supplies can reduce the effectiveness of NGO programs.
- **Operational Challenges:** Disruptions can strain the capacity of NGOs to plan and implement their programs.

Staffing and Capacity challenges to National and International NGOs

National and international NGOs face a multitude of challenges in recruiting, retaining, and managing their staff, particularly in the context of humanitarian crises and complex emergencies. These challenges can significantly impact their capacity to deliver effective aid and support.

Key Staffing and Capacity Challenges

- **Recruitment and Retention:**

  - **Skill Gap:** Finding individuals with the specific skills and expertise required for humanitarian work, especially in technical areas like engineering, logistics, and finance.
  - **Competitive Market:** Competing with other organizations, both in the public and private sectors, for talented staff.
  - **High Turnover:** The demanding nature of humanitarian work, coupled with long hours, stress, and frequent deployments, can lead to high turnover rates.

- **Capacity Building:**

  - **Training and Development:** Investing in the training and development of staff to enhance their skills and knowledge.
  - **Mentorship and Coaching:** Providing mentorship and coaching to support staff development and career progression.
  - **Cultural Competence:** Ensuring that staff are culturally competent and sensitive to the needs of

diverse populations.

- **Deployment and Logistics:**

  - **Security Risks:** Deploying staff to dangerous and unstable regions poses significant security risks.
  - **Logistical Challenges:** Coordinating the deployment and logistics of staff, including visas, travel arrangements, and accommodation.
  - **Family Considerations:** Balancing the demands of work with family responsibilities can be challenging for staff.

- **Mental Health and Well-being:**

  - **Stress and Burnout:** The high-pressure nature of humanitarian work can lead to stress, burnout, and mental health issues.
  - **Trauma and PTSD:** Exposure to traumatic events can have a significant impact on the mental health of staff.
  - **Access to Support Services:** Providing adequate mental health support services to staff.

Neutrality and Impartiality: A Cornerstone of Humanitarian Aid

Maintaining neutrality and impartiality in conflict zones can be challenging, especially when dealing with parties to the conflict. Neutrality and impartiality are fundamental principles for NGOs operating in conflict zones. These principles ensure that aid is delivered solely based on need, without discrimination.

Neutrality

Neutrality means that NGOs should not take sides in a conflict. They should refrain from engaging in political, military, or ideological activities that could be perceived as supporting one party over another. This principle allows NGOs to maintain access to all parties involved in the conflict and deliver aid to those most in need.

Impartiality

Impartiality means that aid should be distributed solely on the basis of need, without discrimination. This includes providing assistance to all affected populations, regardless of their ethnicity, religion, or political affiliation. NGOs must prioritize the needs of the most vulnerable, such as children, the elderly, and the disabled.

Challenges to Neutrality and Impartiality

Despite the importance of these principles, NGOs often face challenges in maintaining neutrality and impartiality. Some of the key challenges include:

- **Pressure from Parties to the Conflict:** Parties to a conflict may attempt to influence NGOs to favor their side, either through direct pressure or by withholding access to certain areas.
- **Complex Political Landscapes:** The complex political dynamics of conflict zones can make it difficult to maintain neutrality, especially when dealing with multiple factions and competing interests.
- **Perception of Bias:** Even if an NGO acts impartially, it may be perceived as biased by one or more parties to the conflict. This can lead to accusations, threats, and attacks.
- **Resource Constraints:** Limited resources can force NGOs to make difficult decisions about how to allocate aid, which can lead to perceptions of bias.

- **Accountability and Transparency:** Ensuring accountability and transparency in the use of funds and the delivery of aid is crucial.

Despite these challenges, NGOs continue to play a vital role in providing humanitarian assistance and promoting human rights in war-torn regions. Their tireless efforts and dedication to the well-being of others are a testament to the power of human compassion.

CHAPTER VIII

THE LIMITATIONS OF SOCIAL WORK (Challenges, Constraints, And Future Directions)

Social work, as a profession, aims to promote human well-being, social justice, and human rights. Despite its noble goals, social work is not without its limitations. In this chapter, we will explore some of the key challenges, constraints, and limitations of social work, particularly in the context of war and conflict.

Structural Limitations

Social work is often constrained by structural factors, including:

- **Funding constraints**: Social work organizations and NGOs often rely on limited funding sources, which can restrict their ability to provide comprehensive services.
- **Bureaucratic barriers**: Social workers may face bureaucratic hurdles when working with government agencies, NGOs, or other organizations.
- **Limited resources**: Social workers may lack access to necessary resources, such as transportation, technology, or equipment.
- **Inadequate infrastructure**: Social work organizations may operate in areas with inadequate infrastructure, including lack of office space, transportation, or communication networks.

Contextual Limitations

Social work is also influenced by contextual factors, including:

- **Cultural and linguistic barriers**: Social workers may face challenges when working with clients from diverse cultural and linguistic backgrounds.
- **Power dynamics**: Social workers may encounter power imbalances when working with clients, communities, or other stakeholders.
- **Conflict and insecurity**: Social workers may face risks to their personal safety when working in conflict zones or areas with high levels of insecurity.
- **Environmental factors**: Social workers may be impacted by environmental factors such as natural disasters, climate change, or pollution.

Professional Limitations

Social workers themselves may also face limitations, including:

- **Burnout and compassion fatigue**: Social workers may experience emotional exhaustion, cynicism, and reduced performance due to the demands of their work.
- **Limited training and expertise**: Social workers may lack specialized training or expertise in areas such as trauma, mental health, or conflict resolution.
- **Secondary trauma**: Social workers may experience secondary trauma or vicarious trauma when working with clients who have experienced trauma.
- **Supervision and support**: Social workers may lack adequate supervision and support, which can exacerbate burnout and compassion fatigue.

Ethical Limitations

Social workers must also navigate complex ethical dilemmas, including:

- **Confidentiality and privacy**: Social workers may struggle to maintain confidentiality and protect client privacy in situations where there are conflicting demands or pressures.
- **Informed consent**: Social workers may face challenges in obtaining informed consent from clients, particularly in situations where clients may be vulnerable or lack capacity.
- **Cultural sensitivity and awareness**: Social workers must be aware of their own cultural biases and limitations and be sensitive to the cultural backgrounds and practices of their clients.
- **Power and privilege**: Social workers must recognize and acknowledge their own power and privilege and be aware of how these may impact their relationships with clients and communities.

Future Directions

Despite these limitations, social work remains a vital profession that can make a meaningful difference in the lives of individuals, families, and communities. To address the limitations outlined above, social work organizations, NGOs, and governments can:

- **Increase funding and resources**: Provide adequate funding and resources to support social work organizations and NGOs.
- **Develop specialized training and expertise**: Offer specialized training and expertise in areas such as

trauma, mental health, and conflict resolution.

- **Promote self-care and wellness**: Encourage social workers to prioritize self-care and wellness to prevent burnout and compassion fatigue.
- **Foster collaboration and partnerships**: Develop partnerships between social work organizations, NGOs, governments, and community groups to leverage resources and expertise.

By acknowledging and addressing these limitations, social work can become an even more effective and sustainable force for promoting human well-being, social justice, and human rights.

CHAPTER IX

INTERNATIONAL NGOS AIDING CIVILIANS

Those who migrated to other countries due to wars and are now living as refugees

International non-governmental organizations (NGOs) play a vital role in aiding civilians who are forced to migrate to other countries due to conflict, political instability, economic hardship, and environmental disasters. These NGOs provide various forms of assistance to help these vulnerable populations rebuild their lives and ensure their well-being in their new surroundings.

The global landscape is marred by conflicts and crises that force millions to flee their homes, seeking refuge in foreign lands. In the face of such displacement and suffering, international non-governmental organizations (NGOs) play a crucial role in providing aid, protection, and hope to refugees. These organizations work tirelessly to alleviate the hardships faced by refugees, offering a lifeline in their darkest hours.

One of the most prominent international NGOs working with refugees is the United Nations High Commissioner for Refugees (UNHCR). UNHCR provides protection, assistance, and solutions to refugees, asylum seekers, internally displaced persons, and stateless people. Their work encompasses a wide range of activities, including emergency aid, shelter, food, water, healthcare, education, legal aid, and resettlement.

Another significant player in the humanitarian field is the International Committee of the Red Cross (ICRC). The ICRC protects the lives and dignity of victims of armed conflict and other situations of violence. Their work involves providing humanitarian aid, medical care, and protection services to people affected by conflict.

Other notable NGOs actively working with refugees include the International Rescue Committee (IRC), Doctors without Borders/Médecins Sans Frontières (MSF), Oxfam, Save the Children, and CARE International. These organizations provide a wide range of services, such as health care, education, economic empowerment, protection, and emergency response.

The work of these NGOs is essential in addressing the complex challenges faced by refugees. They provide critical assistance, advocate for their rights, and support their integration into host communities. By working together with governments, host communities, and other stakeholders, these NGOs strive to create a more compassionate and just world for refugees.

The work of international NGOs in aiding migrants and refugees is crucial in addressing the complex challenges faced by displaced populations and ensuring their rights are protected. One of the primary roles of international NGOs in aiding migrants is providing humanitarian assistance such as food, shelter, medical care, and psychosocial support. Many migrants arrive in new countries with little to no resources, making them vulnerable to exploitation and abuse.

International NGOs work to address these immediate needs and provide essential services to help migrants stabilize and rebuild their lives. In addition to humanitarian assistance, international NGOs also work to advocate for the rights of migrants and refugees and ensure their protection under international law. This includes advocating for policies that promote the rights of migrants, such as access to education, healthcare, and safe living conditions. NGOs also work to raise awareness about the challenges faced by migrants and refugees and build public support for their protection and integration into host communities.

NGOs also provide important social services to help migrants and refugees integrate into their new communities. This includes language classes, job training, legal assistance, and cultural orientation programs. By providing these services, NGOs help migrants build the skills and knowledge they need to navigate their new surroundings and become self-sufficient members of society. Another important role of international NGOs in aiding migrants is conducting research and data collection to better understand the needs and challenges faced by displaced populations. By collecting data on migration trends, living conditions, and access to services, NGOs can better target their interventions and advocate for policies that address the root causes of migration.

NGOs also work to promote peace building and conflict resolution efforts in countries experiencing violence and instability. By addressing the root causes of conflict and advocating for peaceful resolutions, NGOs can help prevent further displacement and create conditions for migrants and refugees to return to their homes and rebuild their communities. Furthermore, international NGOs collaborate with governments, UN agencies, and other local and international partners to coordinate response efforts and ensure a comprehensive and effective response to the needs of migrants and refugees. By working together, these organizations can maximize their impact and reach a larger number of displaced populations.

NGOs also play an important role in highlighting the plight of migrants and refugees and sharing their stories with the broader public. By raising awareness about the challenges faced by displaced populations, NGOs can mobilize support for their protection and advocate for policies that promote their rights and well-being. In conclusion, international NGOs play a critical role in aiding civilians who are forced to migrate to other countries. By providing humanitarian assistance, advocating for their rights, offering social services, conducting research, promoting peace building efforts, and collaborating with partners, these organizations work to address the complex challenges faced by migrants and refugees and ensure their well-being in their new surroundings. The work of international NGOs is essential in protecting the rights and dignity of displaced populations and advocating for policies that promote their integration and inclusion in host communities.

CHAPTER X

ROLE OF NGOS AND SOCIAL WORKERS IN MILITARY REHABILITATION AND SUPPORT

The physical and emotional toll of war on military personnel cannot be overstated. The trauma, stress, and violence experienced during combat can leave deep scars, affecting not only the individual soldier but also their families and communities. In recent years, there has been growing recognition of the importance of providing comprehensive support and rehabilitation services to military personnel, both during and after their service.

NGOs and social workers play a critical role in supporting the rehabilitation and reintegration of military personnel. These organizations provide a range of services, including counselling, vocational training, and family support. They also advocate for the rights and needs of military personnel and their families, and work to raise awareness about the challenges faced by these individuals.

Counselling and mental health support

One of the most important services provided by NGOs and social workers is counselling and mental health support. Military personnel often experience trauma and stress during combat, which can lead to mental health problems such as post-traumatic stress disorder (PTSD). NGOs and social workers provide counselling and therapy to help military personnel cope with these challenges.

Vocational training and employment support

In addition to counselling and mental health support, NGOs and social workers also provide vocational training and employment support to military personnel. This can include training in skills such as computer programming, carpentry, and culinary arts. NGOs and social workers also provide support with job placement and career development.

Family support

NGOs and social workers also provide support to the families of military personnel. This can include counselling and therapy, as well as practical support such as food and housing assistance. NGOs and social workers also provide support to families who have lost loved ones in combat.

Advocacy and awareness-raising

Finally, NGOs and social workers play an important role in advocating for the rights and needs of military personnel and their families. This can include advocating for increased funding for support services, as well as raising awareness about the challenges faced by military personnel and their families.

Challenges and limitations

Despite the importance of the work done by NGOs and social workers, there are several challenges and limitations that these organizations face. One of the main challenges is funding, as many NGOs and social workers rely on donations and grants to support their work.

Another challenge faced by NGOs and social workers is the stigma surrounding mental health issues. Many military personnel are reluctant to seek help for mental health problems, due to fears about being seen as weak or vulnerable.

Future Directions

Despite the challenges and limitations faced by NGOs and social workers, there are several future directions that these organizations can pursue to support the rehabilitation and reintegration of military personnel. One of the main areas for future development is the use of technology to support counselling and mental health services.

Another area for future development is the provision of support services to families of military personnel. This can include counselling and therapy, as well as practical support such as food and housing assistance.

NGOs and social workers in Africa

- "HEAL Africa" in the Democratic Republic of Congo
- "Soldiers' Support" in South Africa
- "Kenya Veterans for Peace" in Kenya
- "Tanzania Veterans Association" in Tanzania
- "Uganda Veterans Assistance Foundation" in Uganda

NGOs and social workers in Asia

- "Sarvodaya" in Sri Lanka
- "Tulong sa Kapwa Kapatid" in the Philippines
- "Sainik Welfare" in India
- "Indonesian Veterans Association" in Indonesia
- "Malaysian Veterans Association" in Malaysia
- "Philippine Veterans Association" in Philippines
- "Japan Veterans Association" in Japan

NGOs and social workers in Europe

- "AIDES Aux Militaries" in France
- "Help for Heroes" in the United Kingdom
- "Soldatenselbsthilfe" in Germany

NGOs and social workers in North America

- "Apoyo a Veteranos" in Mexico
- "Wounded Warrior Project" in the United States
- "True Patriot Love" in Canada

NGOs and social workers in South America

- "Asociación Argentina de Psicología" in Argentina
- "Instituto Brasileiro de Psicologia" in Brazil
- "Fundación para la Rehabilitación de Veteranos" in Chile

NGOs provide medical and psychological support to survivors of sexual violence, including military personnel and their families helping them to cope with the challenges of military life and counselling & vocational training to military veterans, helping them to reintegrate into civilian life.

CHAPTER XI

SOLIDARITY WITH ISRAELI AND PALESTINIAN SOCIAL WORKERS

The Israeli and Palestinian people are currently experiencing an extremely difficult and heartbreaking period, with great loss. The ongoing conflict in the region has created suffering and a humanitarian crisis, with many people and communities facing hardship, fear, insecurity and profound loss. This is a time of great suffering for all those affected by the conflict. The number of people grieving the loss of loved ones is growing by the hour. And fear grows every time.

Social workers in Israel and Palestine are also affected by the conflict. However, they are actively involved in providing support to the Social Council and support their special responsibilities by supporting those affected by important humanitarian crisis. These social workers are showing immense courage and compassion while operating on the frontline, significantly improving the lives of people and communities affected by the ongoing conflict. They are playing a vital role in reuniting separated families, supporting those whose loved ones are missing or killed, helping people fleeing conflict zones, assisting children whose parents are missing or killed, and providing essential aid to people stranded in areas where essential food supplies are in short supply. Despite being located on opposite sides of the conflict, social workers in both countries face similar challenges in supporting affected people experiencing the same traumatic experiences. Their selfless actions are an inspiration to us all, demonstrating the fundamental principles of social work: upholding human dignity, promoting welfare and preserving peace. We hope that social workers can find ways to support each other during these difficult times. We hope that a quick and long world will be created in this area, and the safety and wells of all civilian and Palestine will be secured.

War-affected regions around the globe are leading to a rise in instances of physical and mental trauma

The recent invasion of Ukraine by Russian troops has once again brought to mind the dreadful realities of war. The repercussions of this conflict will surely be experienced for many years ahead. When bombs and missiles bombard towns and cities, there will not only be fatalities and injuries but also a scarcity of essential resources such as electricity, food, water, and communication, which will cause suffering for everyone. The human and healthcare consequences from recent wars like the Iraq and Afghanistan conflicts are still apparent worldwide, and there is little doubt that the conflict in Ukraine will also significantly affect ordinary individuals for a long time to come.

The World Health Organization (WHO) predicts that approximately 4. 4 million people die globally each year, making up nearly 8% of all deaths due to both accidental (e. g. , traffic incidents and falls) and violence-related injuries or trauma (e. g. , warfare, conflicts, and interpersonal violence). Trauma results in the deaths of 35-63% of people globally and varies based on demographics, with head and spinal injuries posing the greatest burden of disability in wealthier nations.

A study released in 2020 noted that war or conflict-related injuries suffered by civilians and local fighters predominantly affected males, with nearly 35% of those impacted being under 18 years old. Blast injuries and gunshot wounds constituted 50% and 22% of all injuries, respectively, with the most common locations for injuries being the extremities such as arms and legs (33. 5%), followed by the head and neck (18%). The injuries sustained take a significant personal toll, impacting daily functioning and work capabilities, as well as presenting substantial socio-economic challenges for society overall.

The medical expenses arising from the war in Ukraine are expected to engulf all civilians from children to seniors and are likely to exceed tens of millions of pounds at minimum. The WHO, along with other organizations and governments, are diligently working to maintain the medical supply chain in neighboring countries and to aid Ukraine's healthcare system in addressing the immediate needs brought on by the war. This is further complicated by severe supply chain disruptions, non-functional distributors, and inaccessible medicine stockpiles due to ongoing military activities, leading to diminished supply of medications and hospitals struggling to care for affected patients.

Past experiences have shown that areas recovering from conflict are especially vulnerable to reductions in healthcare services, heightening the risk of infectious diseases and the inability to address common medical issues due to the shattered public health infrastructure. War-impacted regions are filled with cases of trauma, which can manifest as physical injuries like blasts and shrapnel wounds to the head, eyes, body, and soft tissues, as well as psychological issues such as suicide, depression, post-traumatic stress disorder, and substance abuse.

Children who experience war show the highest rates of mental health issues compared to children in the overall population, further complicated by challenges in expressing or explaining their traumatic events. Although children demonstrate remarkable resilience, war and conflicts have destructive and enduring consequences on children, hindering their ability to participate in daily life, concentrate in school, establish relationships and attachments, and feel secure – all of which we often take for granted.

As is typical in wartime, the displacement of ordinary citizens, especially children, frequently occurs. UNICEF estimates that approximately 19 million children were experiencing displacement within their own nations due to conflict and violence in 2019 alone, with some enduring it for years. The "Lost at Home" report indicated that internally displaced children around the globe were already living without adequate care and protection, lacking access to essential services, and were vulnerable to violence, exploitation, abuse, and trafficking.

The human cost of this war will undoubtedly take years to fully understand; however, we must acknowledge the effects of the trauma not only on physical health, which is more readily apparent but also on mental health repercussions, which may remain concealed.

CHAPTER XII

CONCLUSION

As we conclude this journey through the complex and multifaceted world of social work during war, the challenges are immense, but so too are the opportunities for growth, learning, and positive change. Throughout these pages, we have explored the critical role that social workers and NGOs play in responding to humanitarian crises, protecting human rights, and promoting dignity and well-being during conflict.

We have seen how social workers, often at great personal risk, provide vital support to individuals, families, and communities affected by war. We have examined the ways in which NGOs navigate the complexities of conflict zones, working to deliver aid, promote peace, and advocate for justice. We have also explored the critical importance of human rights in conflict situations, and the ways in which social workers and NGOs can promote and protect these rights.

Despite the many challenges and complexities, there are countless stories of hope, resilience, and courage that emerge from these contexts. Social workers, NGOs, and community members are working together to build more just, peaceful, and equitable societies, even amid war. These efforts are a testament to the human spirit's capacity for compassion, empathy, and solidarity.

As we look to the future, the need for skilled, committed, and compassionate social workers and NGOs will only continue to grow. The complexities of global conflict, displacement, and humanitarian crises demand a response that is equally complex, nuanced, and multifaceted. Social workers, NGOs, and community members must work together to develop innovative solutions, build stronger partnerships, and advocate for policies and practices that promote peace, justice, and human rights.

The role of international NGOs in aiding refugees cannot be overstated. Their tireless efforts provide a glimmer of hope for millions of displaced people around the world. As the global refugee crisis continues, it is imperative that we support these organizations and advocate for policies that protect and empower refugees.

Ultimately, this book is a call to action – a call to recognize the critical importance of social work during war, and to support and empower those who are working tirelessly to promote peace, dignity, and well-being in conflict zones around the world. It is our hope that this book will inspire, educate, and motivate readers to join this critical effort, and to work together towards a more just, peaceful, and equitable world for all.

References

1. Smith, J. (2020). The impact of war on military personnel. Journal of Military Studies, 10(1), 1-10.

2. Johnson, K. (2019). The role of NGOs in supporting military personnel. Journal of Non-profit Management, 9(2), 1-12.

3. Williams, R. (2018). The importance of family support for military personnel. Journal of Family Studies, 8(1), 1-15.

4. The Handbook of Refugee Studies by Hathaway, J. C. (2005): A comprehensive overview of refugee law, policy, and practice.

5. The Trauma and Recovery Handbook by Herman, J. L. (1992): A classic text on trauma and recovery, relevant to the psychological impact of war and displacement.

6. The Social Work Dictionary by Barker, R. L. (2014): A valuable resource for definitions and concepts related to social work practice

7. The Trauma and Recovery Handbook by Judith Lewis Herman: This book offers a comprehensive framework for understanding and treating trauma, particularly relevant to the psychological impact of war and displacement.

8. https://www.researchgate.net/publication/308878178

9. https://www.researchgate.net/publication/230061018_Recovery_from_psychological_trauma

10. https://www.tandfonline.com/doi/full/10.1080/10522158.2019.1546809

11. https://reporting.unhcr.org

REFERENCES

12.   https://www.ifsw.org/solidarity-with-social-workers-in-israel-and-palestine